Ten

Grief

Lessons

From Golf

Robin Chodak

Table of Contents

Dedication

I dedicate this book to my late husband Dr. Gerald Chodak.

He was the one who introduced me to the game of golf, and

I am grateful for what I have learned from him. He loved it

and played as often as he could, especially when he retired.

He lived his life always doing what he loved even until his

last day on this earth. His last round of golf was played on

the day he died 9/28/19. Gerry's zest for golf and the game

of life has been an inspiration to all who knew him. May

we all embrace the love for life that he had and live it to the

fullest.

Acknowledgments

A big thank you to my friend Del DeMao who inspired me to play the game of golf with passion after my husband Gerry died. I learned how to have fun playing golf with him. I also thank Ricky Palonis for the golf tips he gave me and the great conversations we had about golf and life. I wish him much success in his golf career. Thank you Katie Abbott for the invaluable edits to this book.

Introduction

This book came to fruition from a nudge from divine spirit just as all my other books have been written. One day while meditating on a PEMF (pulsed electromagnetic field) therapy mat for my back pain, I heard "the voice" in my head, which I've heard many times in my life. It said, "Write another book about grief and how it's related to golf." It made sense because I couldn't play golf due to my back pain, thus the reason for using the PEMF mat.

It's not by chance that the date was January 11, 2022, when I heard the message. If you have read any of my books or blogs, you know that I align with the energetic power of numbers. Number 1 is a master number that holds great power. At least it does for me; since 2006 I have been guided by the number 11. Many significant things have happened on 11/11 days for me or at the time 11:11. I see 11:11 on the clock every day. I write about it in my book,

"Three Must Have Connections for Inner Peace," available on Amazon.

When I heard the voice in my meditation, I knew I needed to heed the call.

It's not by any remote surprise that this came to me because in November, upon my annual return to Florida my intention was to improve my golf game. I said to myself, *why not? I live on a golf course. It seems logical to take advantage of it while living here. I don't know how long I will stay!* I knew as a grief coach that the griever should not make any decisions for at least one year. I am not talking about buying a new piece of clothing or starting golf lessons. I am referring to situations that will cause your life to change in a significant way, such as moving to a new location. Those big decisions can often affect your finances as well. It's important to hold off on them until you are certain of your financial situation and sometimes, it may take years. I decided that while I live on the golf course, I shall play as often as I can! Thankfully my back is healed and I can do so.

If you're like me, you believe things happen for a reason and it's all about timing. I met my second husband Steve at a golf course on the first day of a group lesson in 1995.

Interestingly, I never continued golf, but that was the predecessor for meeting my third husband, Gerry after Steve died. I am where I am today mentally and spiritually because of all my experiences and relationships. I have learned it's important to seize the moments you are given in this physical realm as often as you can—they never return. None of us are promised anything in our future. Playing golf continues to show me its analogies to grief. I hope this book will inspire you on your journey through grief, regardless of whether you play golf or not. In this book, I will tell you ten reasons why playing the game of golf is like experiencing grief and the lessons to be learned.

Chapter 1: My Story

Don't run away from grief, o' soul/ Look for the remedy inside the pain/ because the rose came from the thorn/ and the ruby came from a stone.

~Rumi

I want to share some of my story with you. At the time of this writing, it's been two years and three months since my husband Gerry passed away in our home in Michiana Shores, Indiana. His day started out great for him. He had an early morning tee time. He was an avid golfer and loved the game. Actually, he was a scratch golfer, which means he could play to a course handicap of zero on all rated golf courses.

Scratch golfers can manage every aspect of their game consistently and can plot their way around the golf course hitting the right shots at the right time. They very rarely hit two bad shots in a row and have the mindset to recover rapidly from setbacks in a positive way. I certainly witnessed it with Gerry. In fact, he won three championships at three different Golf Country Clubs. He was known as the *best chipper* in the club. It didn't matter if the ball was 10 ft. or 30 ft. away from the pin, he would often chip it in the hole. Golfers named his ability the "Chodak Chip" and they wanted to emulate it themselves. Many golfers asked him to teach them; it wasn't uncommon to find him on the course instructing someone how to do chip shots. He was always willing to help. He found great joy in watching others hit great shots and improve their golf game.

During the golf game on September 28, 2019, Gerry complained to his foursome about a stomachache; yet, he finished the round. It's normal for Gerry to push himself no matter what the situation. When he arrived home he went straight to the couch for a nap.

My brother, Randy, planned an overnight visit to our

house to help with some handyman things. He was always willing to help whenever I needed electrical or carpentry work done—always a top-notch job.

That evening at our golf country club, Randy, Gerry, and I enjoyed good food, wine, and conversation. Gerry seemed his *chipper* self and engaged in conversation with another golf member. He didn't complain or exhibit any signs of stomach pain. The evening deluged us with rain by the time we finished dinner. Gerry offered to walk one of the elderly members to her car with his umbrella. He was that type of guy, one who was always willing to help someone and often went out of his way to do so. It was one of the qualities that made him a great doctor and a great human.

We arrived home and sat on the enclosed front porch watching the storm on Lake Michigan. It's a spectacular show to watch flashes of light spontaneously light up the sky over the lake while hearing the sound of rumbling thunder. We enjoyed it immensely, and I watched Gerry look out into the vastness. I remember his words—"This is remarkable." A few minutes later, I went to bed. Randy made his way to the bedroom in the basement, and Gerry changed into his robe and made his way to the living room couch. He loved to unwind at night before bed by playing a few games of online chess on his Mac laptop. He was an excellent chess player and so is his son David. They often enjoyed the game together over the Internet.

Nothing seemed unusual on this night. I cuddled in my comfy bed listening to the pouring rain hit the windowpane. I yelled to Gerry, "I love you," and he said the same back. The nights Gerry came to bed later than me, he'd always kiss my forehead before falling into sleep. I always acknowledged his kiss, even in my sleep state. But, this night, I didn't get the kiss. Instead, at 2:30 a.m. my iPhone woke me with an amber alert. I made my way to the kitchen to turn it off. In the darkness of the night, I saw

Gerry sleeping in an upright position on the couch. He looked peaceful, I didn't wake him. I dimmed the Himalayan salt lamp that sat on the kitchen counter. He often thought it was too bright—he loved the pure darkness. I knew once he awoke he would find his way to the bedroom. He often came to bed at unusual hours.

After I silenced my phone, I crawled back into bed. I slept for approximately two more hours then suddenly awoke around 4:30 a.m. realizing Gerry wasn't in the bed. A strange feeling rushed over me and I abruptly jumped out of bed calling his name while I made my way to the living room. He looked in the same peaceful state he was in just a few hours before. In the darkness, I tapped his shoulder and said, "Gerry, come to bed." He didn't move. I did it again, but still no movement. The next time was more forceful. There was only stillness and darkness. I touched his face— it was ice cold. It was then that a wailing sound emerged from my being with words inaudible. I was in shock. It was a moment I never wanted to relive. I lived it before, in 2005, when I found my husband Steve dead in our basement from self-inflicted gunshots to his head. At that time, I thought I'd never recover—that is another story that is not meant for this book.

My screeching sounds continued and woke my brother. My neighbors heard me from their house and ran to mine. We were all very much in shock. *How could Gerry be dead?* He was the most active, fit, healthy, happy guy we all knew. He was our inspiration, but now he was suddenly gone. Poof—into thin air—just like Steve. Yet, my life continued.

How could this happen? This must be another cruel joke played on me. I already lost a husband and a sister. Plus, I am a grief coach. I have a business helping people with their grief. Something in the universe must be amiss.

Grief continues to give me opportunities to learn and grow. It teaches me to live with a heart full of gratitude and to learn to love others and myself more. It allows me to live my purpose, which is to help you on your journey. You may even improve your golf game!

Chapter 2: Why Grief is Like Golf

S O why am I writing about grief and golf? It's because I have personal experience with both. I tried many different sports and activities in my life, such as tennis, pickleball, volleyball, yoga, and dancing, yet golf seemed to be the hardest. I couldn't understand why the little golf ball had so much control over me. Until you learn how to manage the game it will control you. Grief is no different. You must learn how to manage it. When you lose someone you love, you never get over the grief you experience. Instead, what I say is that *you learn to integrate the pain into your life.* The word *integrate* means to combine one thing with another so it can become whole. That is the goal after experiencing any type of loss. You combine it with *who you will become* as you strive to be whole. In other words, you don't let the loss define you. It becomes an integral part of who you are, and you evolve into the person you are today because of it.

Every choice you've made is a culmination of who you are

today. And every choice you make from this day forward is

creating your future. So choose wisely.

You can learn a lot about a person while you watch

them play the game of golf. All genders play golf, but for

simplicity's sake, I'm going to use (he) while I refer to the

golfer. Next time you're watching a golfer play, ask

yourself the following questions. Does he get angry with

himself when he hits a bad shot? Does he react to his bad

shot by doing something physical such as throwing the club

or banging his fist, etc? Does he yell profanity? Does he

reach for a drink or a smoke? Does his body language

change? Do you see him tighten up while he takes his next

swing? This is not to say that the golfer can't change any

bad habits he may have. He certainly can if he is committed

to the game. In time, he will learn that those negative

behaviors only hinder his game, not help it. Perhaps the

golfer is calm, cool, and collective. All of his reactions to every part of the game reveal his character. It's a metaphor for how he lives his own life.

Interestingly, golf is a valuable tool for companies looking to hire high-level executives. My friend Gary told me that he invites his potential hires to play a round of golf with him. **Why?** It gives him insight into the person's character beyond the interview process. It makes a lot of sense to me because golf speaks volumes about someone's personality. For example, Gary will observe if the person exhibits anger while playing. He can determine if he is competitive or not. He watches how the person interacts with others. He gets answers to the following questions. How does he dress—in the proper attire? Does he exhibit golf etiquette? Does he follow the course rules? Is he grateful to his competitors? Is he polite? One that he pays special attention to is whether the person cheats at his own game. If he does, it's a telltale warning sign! All of the person's behaviors on the course will most likely be carried into his work. Gary wants to hire a man with ethical behaviors, and the golf game assists him.

There are many things you will discover about a person while they play the game of golf. It's brilliant! Perhaps anyone looking for a serious relationship should play golf with his or her potential partner!

It's the same with grief. You can learn a lot about a grieving person based on how they respond to it. A person either grows from the grief experience or they stay stuck in it and play the victim role. It's really their choice.

Grievers often feel like the golfer because they don't know why grief has so much power over them. The reason is that they have loved. The more you love, the more you shall grieve. Think about it. If you lose something that's not important, it doesn't have a big impact on you, but if it has a sentimental value it certainly will. After my husband, Gerry died, I lost an earring he gave me down my bathroom sink drain. I was sick about it and asked my neighbor, Neal, to take the sink apart. Fortunately, he found it. If it didn't mean anything to me, it wouldn't have mattered if I lost it.

Grief has been ever-present in my life starting at a young age. I tell my story in my book, "Be Gentle with Me, I'm Grieving," but I will also tell it here briefly.

My father was not very present during my childhood, therefore my three siblings and I were left alone much of the time. My parents had a tumultuous relationship, and my father came and went. It left my mom in a challenging position. When I was two, my dad left my mom, and she had to move back home with her parents. My grandmother babysat me while my mom worked in department stores and restaurants so she could support me. Sadly, my grandmother died when I was three. My mom didn't have much of a support system, yet she was resilient. Thankfully, I inherited that quality from her. My dad left his family for good when I was twelve. I longed for a father figure; therefore it's not a surprise that I became pregnant at 15. The boy was three years older than me, and we married one month after my 16th birthday. As a mother at that age, I lost the experience of living my teenage years. That is another story that could be its own book that I may write one day!

At that time in my life, it would have been easy to play the victim role, but I didn't let my predicament hold me down. Yes, my life was certainly harder than most at 16 with a husband and baby, but I kept pushing myself to grow and evolve. It took a lot of work on my part. I wanted to succeed in life then, just as I want to succeed at golf today.

Chapter 3: Golf is too Hard

You believe golf is too hard, and you are not alone in saying it. I and so many others have said, "I don't want to continue to do it" after the frustration of playing. During grief, you may believe the same. You believe it's too hard and you don't want to do it! You want to give up. You may want to harm yourself unconsciously by drinking, eating, spending money, or self-sabotaging in other ways. Those are the reasons many people get into stuck states—they don't want to do *it*. Doing *it* means processing your grief. As a grief coach, I help you learn how to process your grief. I have online courses and books to help you do so. For more information, visit my website at www.robinchodak.com.

As a beginner golfer, you really don't know what to expect. You don't know how it's going to impact you mentally or physically until you begin. You don't even know what your body needs to do to help you play the game. It's the same with grief. Your body doesn't know what to do when it goes into shock from a traumatic loss. I experienced it twice when my husbands died. The physical body must learn how to recover. It must have proper rest and a healthy diet. There are modalities such as; meditation, massage, Reiki, acupuncture, and many more that help the body heal. It needs to be taken care of while it's grieving. It's just like golf because a golfer must do the same to prepare for a game or tournament. They must take care of their body and their mind. They must eat the proper foods, hydrate, have a positive mental attitude, and have the body stretched and relaxed.

In golf, one of the first things you must learn is to get into the right stance to prepare for the swing. In other words, you need to learn how to stand properly.

After a loss, you must learn how to stand on your own, without your loved one. I refer to loss in this book as the death of a loved one, but grief is experienced from so much more. It can be the loss of a particular experience, a pet, a job, a home, your health, etc. Grief is the feeling of separation from something that was once familiar to you. Once it's gone, you are left with feelings of emptiness or sometimes no hope at all. **Have you felt like that?** I certainly did. What did you do to help yourself? Think about your answers and write them down. I am a firm believer in writing things down on paper. It will help you remember and reflect on your answers.

While you read this book, make the analogy with your own loss. Getting yourself into the right stance is really about creating a new identity. Each and every loss is different. Each time, you must learn how to re-invent yourself. After the tragic suicide of my husband Steve, I was no longer a wife of a politician, guitar player, father, and husband. I had to recover from the traumatic event and also the stigma of suicide that was monumental at that time. Today there is much more awareness about it. I had to learn how to stand on my own and create a new identity. Thankfully, I found support, which was hard to do in 2005. The loss eventually led me to become trained by AFSP (American Foundation for Suicide Prevention) as a group facilitator. It also paved the way for me to become a writer and start my grief coaching business.

In golf it's the same; you must learn your stance. If you don't get your body positioned in the right direction and form it will affect your results. For example, as you prepare for your *tee shot*, if your stance is not correct, the ball won't go straight down the fairway. If you're like me, you practice at the range hitting many balls. After most of them haven't gone straight I realize it's my position. The ball responds when contact is made. The direction is determined by the positioning of your feet to it. There are other aspects of the swing that are important that will determine the direction, such as clubface positioning.

It's the same with grief. Metaphorically, you think you

are standing properly to keep you moving in the right direction until something happens to show you otherwise. It happens to let you know you need to make a change in the direction you are headed. Did you veer to the right or the left? Are you off the course from where you want to be headed in life after your loss? You must have your feet pointed in the direction of where you want to go. A Buddha quote says it all, "If you are facing in the right direction, all you need to do is keep on walking."

It's important to have small achievable goals. It might be something as simple as joining a book club or signing up for golf lessons! Golf is no different; you control the direction of your shot by how you stand. Believe me, it takes a long time to get it right. That's the reason I say, *the game of golf is like grief.*

It is normal to take steps in the wrong direction as you put your life back together after loss. Perhaps you started a job too soon, or started a relationship and later realized it was wrong. Don't give up, it's part of the process to help you learn and make better choices. It's the same with golf; you don't give up. **Why?** Because deep down you want to achieve a measured level of success. In golf, you acknowledge your successes and wins, and that keeps you coming back to the game. I know when I hit a great chip shot close to the pin, it makes me feel awesome! I want to stay in the game with the hope of doing it again. It's even better when you can chip one in—I have done it! It's the same with grief; when you have a positive outcome, you will want to do it again. An example is to attend a grief/loss support group. You found it helpful, so you tried it again.

I will give you my example. For 12 years my husband and I lived in Florida seven months out of the year, and when I returned the first year after he died I was very lonely. It was during the pandemic, yet Florida wasn't in strict 'lockdown,' therefore people continued to dine out.

Even though I knew going out alone would be hard, out of desperation I decided to do it for the first time as a widowed woman. To my surprise, it wasn't as bad as I thought, and I had some enjoyable conversations. So I did it again. It takes courage to go out alone if that is something you haven't been accustomed to doing in the past. Creating your new identity is all about putting yourself *out there* and stretching yourself to do things you haven't done before. You will find that you have more strength than you thought you had. It's the same with golf—put yourself *out there*. Stretch yourself by doing things new. For me, it was to play in a nine and dine outing. I never wanted to do it because I lacked confidence in my game. I had to stretch myself to do it and I am glad I did. **What was the result?** I had fun and met Mary. We began to golf together regularly, and it helped me improve. If I didn't stretch myself beyond my limited thinking, it wouldn't have happened.

Grief is no different than golf; you might go for years

and feel like you're moving forward and everything is seemingly good and then *wham!* Your game (grief) goes to sh*t. Either some event or another loss triggers you back into grieving. That's when it's important to get a coach or some type of support system. Remember, seeking help is not a sign of weakness, nor does it mean that you have forgotten everything you have learned. It means you are human and need a little jumpstart again!

Lesson to be learned: Don't think grief is too hard; you can process it just as you can learn to play golf. What needs to be done is to understand it and find the right resources to help you.

Chapter 4: There's no Improvement

You don't see improvement in your golf game, even after some time has passed, and you don't believe you ever will. This is a very common theme for beginner golfers. It gets very frustrating for them because they spend hours upon hours at the range hitting balls. As a golfer, you try to implement everything you have learned, and yet there is no improvement. There are many pieces to the puzzle when it comes to the game of golf. There's the grip, the stance, the position of the feet, the weight of your body and how it moves during the swing, and the follow-through after contact with the ball. It's important to put all those pieces together in the proper way to execute the results you want.

Most people want to be good at what they do, and they measure themselves by their improvement. You may be very good at tennis and thought it would be the same with golf, but when you started it you discovered you weren't. You become frustrated because you expected to be just as good at it with no effort. That is where the problem lies. You thought it should have been automatic and would take little effort. Wow, did you get a rude awakening! It was the same for me, and I found it to be a very humbling experience.

I believe things come into our lives to keep the *ego* in check. You must realize you can't improve or have success without effort. For example, this book and my three others would not have been written if I didn't take the time and commitment to work on them. It took much effort on my part. Just as working through grief and playing golf do! There is no magic pill to do it for you. But there is a magic formula! Everyone has access to it—**commitment** and **effort**.

The question is: ***do you want to see improvement in***

your golf game? If you answered, *yes,* it shows you're committed, and that is the first step. The next step is— make it happen. **How do you do it?** You begin the process and set attainable goals for yourself, such as setting a regular schedule to practice. It's important to focus on one thing at a time. You want your head to be clear. For example, if you find you have a problem with your balance, focus on that for the day. The next time, focus on the movement of your hips during the swing. Take every aspect of the swing and focus only on that one thing until you feel comfortable and are executing it correctly. Be committed to your schedule!

It's the same question for the griever. **Do you want your life to improve after your loss?** Or do you want to stay in your current negative emotional state? I am referring to stuck states and not the normal stages of grief. According to Kübler-Ross the stages of grief are Denial, Anger, Bargaining, Depression, and Acceptance.

Remember, these are not linear, and you move in and out of them at different times. David Kessler, who co-authored a book with Ross, came up with the 6th stage, "finding meaning." I would also like to add a new stage of grief that I have identified. I believe it's ongoing—you do it as long as you live. It is to keep a connection or a *continuing bond* with your loved ones after they are gone. I would like to be the one to coin "**continuing bond**" as the **7th stage of grief** because I believe, "grief never really goes away; you learn to integrate the pain into your life."

The *continuing bond* concept might seem strange to you, and you may wonder, ***how do you do it?*** There are many ways that you can stay connected, and below are just a few. Do any that feel right for you.

- Write letters to your deceased loved ones.
- Talk to the deceased. I often talk to Gerry and ask him to help me remember the golf tips he gave me.

- Talk about the deceased to new friends or acquaintances that never knew him or her. They can learn about all of their wonderful qualities and your relationship with them. It can help someone understand you better.

Talking about your loved ones helps to keep them alive in your heart and mind.

- Live your life in a way that would make your deceased proud. When I do something I think Steve or Gerry would be proud of, I make sure to tell them and it makes me feel good.

- Keep something that belonged to them. You can't keep everything, but one or two items that hold special meaning can be helpful.

- Find something that your loved one liked to do, and try it out for yourself. You may discover you like it too!

- Pay attention to signs from them. They can show up in many different ways, through numbers, animals, music, smells, etc.

Those are just a few suggestions, and you can come up with your own. Perhaps this doesn't work for you, but if it can help ease your pain and help you to feel connected to your deceased loved one, why not give it a try? They are never really gone. I believe that the energy of your loved one always exists. This poem by Mary Elizabeth Frye agrees.

Do Not Stand At My Grave And Weep

Do not stand at my grave and weep,

I am not there. I do not sleep.

I am a thousand winds that blow;

I am the diamond glints on snow.

I am the sunlight on ripened grain;

I am gentle autumn rain.

When you awaken in the morning's hush,

I am the swift uplifting rush

Of quiet birds in circled flight.

I am the soft stars that shine at night.

Do not stand at my grave and cry.

I am not there I did not die.

If you don't see improvement in your life as you move through the stages of grief, take one thing and focus on it just as you do with your golf swing. It may be the decision to work with a grief coach. It may be to commit to sleeping eight hours a night. Or it may be to begin a healthy diet. There are many things the griever must do to see improvement. It's like golf, you may not see it initially, but it's important to stay committed to your game. And as I said, it does take effort. In grief, you must stay committed to your healing. Ask yourself the following questions and listen for the answers honestly. Then write them on paper.

Look at your answers periodically to access your grief journey.

- Do I believe I deserve to be happy?

- Do I want to be happy?

- Is there something holding me back from being happy?

If you answered *NO* to questions 1 and 2, spend some time asking, ***what is the reason?*** It's normal to feel unhappy initially after a loss and especially a tragic one, but it's not normal in the long term. If you continue to be unhappy, there is an underlying issue that needs revealing. If you know the answer to number 3—that is fantastic! You can begin to unravel what it is and focus on it, just as you do with golf. Focus on one thing at a time. If you don't know the answer to what is holding you back I suggest you work with a professional to help uncover it.

If you believe that you can't improve your golf game

or that you will never be happy after a loss, then those are false beliefs that you unconsciously accepted at some time in your life, usually at a very young age. It's those beliefs that keep you from moving forward or improving your situation. As a grief coach, I help my clients identify the beliefs that they have adopted. During the process, they often discover the beliefs that have held them back. Usually, they weren't even aware of them. Those beliefs automatically controlled them. Remember, every choice you have ever made or will make is governed by your belief system. The same holds true for your responses to situations. You are wired a particular way, and you respond to situations based on your beliefs. Thankfully, your beliefs can be changed!

An example is a man named Rich (all client names have been changed in this book), who begins to play golf for the first time in his 40s. He plays a few times and believes it's too hard and that he won't improve. He wants to give up and says to himself, *I won't be good at it no matter how much I try.* His friend suggested he work with a coach. Rich discovered that *the belief* came when he was very young. Growing up he worked with his dad in the service industry selling produce. He never liked it and wanted something other than that for his life; therefore he wasn't enthused about it. His father was aware of his lack of motivation and often said many times, *you'll never amount to anything; you can't even manage potatoes!* This strongly impacted Rich, and throughout his life, he struggled to succeed at any new job he tried. In his mind, he accepted what his father had said about him, *that he would never amount to anything.* He believed his destiny was selling potatoes because of his failures. Although it was his father's belief, it didn't need to be his! Don't buy into the idea that you can't change. That is another false belief that gets ingrained in your head! You can always change or do things differently if you have the desire to do so!

Rich continued to work with a coach, and things began to change in positive ways for him. A year later he met a woman whose father was an avid golfer and lived in a country club. This allowed Rich the opportunity to play often. Three years later he married the woman, and they moved to her father's golf club. Rich is now a 10 handicap. Initially, his belief tried to keep him stuck! But fortunately, it didn't. It wasn't easy—he had to do the mental work by changing his thoughts along with the physical work. He used the magic formula—**commitment and effort**. Years later, Rich decided to go back into the family produce business, and it became extremely profitable. Rich became a success on many levels. So can you! It happened because he was willing to do the work and let go of his false beliefs.

Lesson to be learned: Don't accept that there will be no improvement in your life. You can always improve! Examine your beliefs. Test them out. Ask; *Are they keeping me stuck?* If so, realize you have the power to change them.

Chapter 5: I Hate Golf

You say you hate the game of golf because it frustrates you more than you thought possible. Hate is a very powerful word that I don't use often due to its negative connotation. Yet I believe there is a reason to hate something, such as, I hate injustice, I hate war, I hate racism, etc. Sometimes we use the word *hate* even for the things we love. At the age of 13, I spewed *I hate you* to my mom because she grounded me. I certainly didn't hate her; I loved her. But my underdeveloped emotions were at work. The result of that encounter was enough for me to never say I hated her again! You may say or think you hate something, but in reality, you don't. I always tell my clients, *be careful of the words you speak because you can never take them back!* I also teach and make it a goal of mine to follow the Four Agreements of Don Miguel Ruiz. The 1st agreement is, "Be Impeccable with Your Word." **What exactly does that mean?** It means to speak with integrity. To say only what you mean.

Avoid using your words to speak against yourself or to

gossip about others. Always use the power of your words in

the direction of truth and love. That is very powerful and

attainable if you begin to practice it. Do you find that you

say negative things about your life and your golf? If you

begin to practice the agreement, over time you will learn

not to speak negative things about yourself or others. The

2nd agreement, "Don't take anything personally" is often

difficult because you worry about what others say and think

about you. But you must realize you can't change their

thoughts or actions. You are the stronger person when you

don't take it to heart and react to situations in a respectful

manner. Don't let others define how you play your game of

life. The 3rd agreement, "Don't make assumptions" applies

to your game just as it applies to any person. You can't

possibly know what the outcome will be of your game or

an experience, therefore don't project any negative

thoughts upon it. If you start out playing golf badly, don't assume it will end badly. If a choice you made during your grief created a bad result, don't assume it will stay that way. The 4th agreement, "Always do your best," applies to life no matter what it is you are doing, whether it's selling potatoes or selling million-dollar homes! Do your best in golf and grief.

Living the four agreements becomes a way of life. Begin to apply them in your golf game and all your experiences, and you will become a much happier person.

You may say you hate golf and never want to play it again. This may be your thinking in the beginning as you try to learn the game. For me, I couldn't believe that the little tiny golf ball had so much effect on me—it was not positive! I would set myself up as taught, go for a swing, and miss the ball entirely! I asked myself, *how could this happen?* What kind of power does this ball have that it decides to do what it wants? I'm in control, yet it just sits there when I swing. It goes left or right when I want it to go straight. It rolls low when it should go high. It has a mind

of its own and I certainly can't find a connection to it! The

ball makes me crazy. I exhaust myself with swing after

swing like a crazy woman because I want to get it right. I

developed a love/hate relationship with it. When I would

finally make contact with the ball and it went straight, I was

euphoric. But then, whammy, the next shot wasn't the same

and made me hate the game all over again. I felt like a yo-

yo going back and forth with my relationship with it.

Wasn't it supposed to be fun? Why was I so hard on

myself?

I learned from my self-reflection that I placed too

much pressure on myself. When I played with my husband,

I wanted to please him. He was an amazing golfer, and I

had a false belief that I would learn it and become good

quickly. And that we would have wonderful experiences

playing together and relishing in my success. Well, did I

have an eye-opener! My problem was my expectations. I

expected to be like him. Or at least someone he could be proud of! In my mind, I thought he would only be proud if I was a good golfer. That was a false belief. Anyone who knew Gerry would attest to that. He was proud of me regardless of the outcome and encouraged me anytime I hit a good shot! The problem was that I put extreme pressure on myself—I couldn't relax and I wasn't having fun. **Have you ever felt the same**? Were you trying to please someone so much that you couldn't relax? Believe it or not, it does affect your game. You must realize that the game is yours; not someone else's—you own it.

Gerry always said I needed to practice to become good and that it would take time. But the truth was I didn't want to give it the time it needed. I wanted to skip that step and get on the course and play well. If you have been golfing for some time, you know it doesn't work that way. I had to make the decision to give it the time it needed with the understanding that it would take me away from other enjoyable things. It's all about choice, but if it's something you really desire you don't mind—you give it the time. Think about how much time the golf pros must put into their practice before a tournament. They had to choose to put the time in, otherwise, they wouldn't have made it to the tournament in the first place. I also believe they are impeccable with their words when it comes to self-talk. I don't believe they have a lot of negative comments running wild in their head during their game. It's the same with grief. You may say you hate your life after your loss. You hate that you must live without your loved one. You hate that all your dreams have been shattered. You may think *the game of life* is too hard just as the golfer may think of the game. But something makes you stay with it. **What is it?** It can be a number of things. For many, it's your children or someone else you care about that keeps you hanging in there after your loved one dies. They give you a reason to stay in the game. It doesn't matter what the reason is—what matters is that you don't give up. If you stay in the game and keep moving forward things will improve. You can't deny the *law of inertia,* also called Newton's first law. It states, that if a body is at rest or moving at a constant speed in a straight line, it will remain at rest or keep moving in a straight line at constant speed unless a force acts upon it. Think about it—couch potatoes tend to stay couch potatoes. Successful people often become more successful, the rich get richer and the happy get happier. It works because they keep the inertia going to create their desired results—so can you!

If you dedicate the time to work on your grief just as a golfer does on the game, it can happen. You must decide that is what you want to do. You may feel like a yo-yo as you move forward because something triggers you to fall back, but this is normal. It shouldn't cause you to think you can't succeed. You must give yourself some grace!

My client Dave lost his wife to suicide after nine years of marriage. Early on in their marriage, his wife Laura was diagnosed with depression. The doctors constantly changed her medication. Her highs and lows made their relationship very volatile. Dave had his own set of challenges. He was a heavy drinker and used Laura's depression as his excuse to drink. The difficult times escalated, and after a night of over-indulgence, Dave was slapped with a DUI. This was a rude awakening for him, and fortunately, it led to his sobriety. The marriage became better after some time had passed. Dave believed his sobriety would help his wife's depression—it didn't. Laura lost all hope in life and tragically died of an intentional overdose. As you can imagine, Dave was distraught and he reached out to me for help. In his mind, he believed he was responsible for his wife's death, which is a common theme related to suicide— an erroneous one.

Initially, after her death he stayed sober, but one night he went out and started to drink again. It led to a weeklong binge. He reached out for help once again. After following the Alcoholics Anonymous 12 steps and processing his grief, he realized that he was not the cause of his wife's death nor was drinking the answer to his problems. Dave needed to give himself grace for falling back into drinking and allowing false beliefs to cloud his mind. Remember, if you take steps backward, it doesn't mean that you can't succeed. What it does mean is that you need to get in the game again. Don't let the one mistake make you believe you are a failure—you're not. Continue to take one step forward and get the help you need.

The topic of suicide is very complex and the example was a brief one. I write more about dealing with grief after suicide in my book, "Be Gentle with Me, I'm Grieving."

A golf example is Tiger Woods—think of the mistakes he has made in his personal life. He was ostracized in the tabloids due to his infidelity. It affected his marriage and his golf game. Yet nothing holds him down. Even after several back operations—he stays in the game.

In the beginning after a loss, you mustn't have expectations that are too high—they must be realistic. This applies also to golf. What matters most is that you move at your own pace—start out slowly.

Working with grief can be a very slow process for some, and that is o.k. For example, if your loss was a tragic one, then perhaps your initial goals are to get out of bed, get dressed and go outside for a walk. These actions may seem quite trite for some, but for you, it may be great progress.

In time, the struggling golfer learns not to hate the game and the griever learns not to hate their life.

Lesson to be learned: Do not hate grief. Allow it to teach you and help you become the best version of yourself. And always stay in the game!

Chapter 6: You Need Someone

You realize you need someone to help you learn the game of golf. It's not an easy game to pick up on your own. Perhaps you seek someone to help you learn the mechanics. I've also noticed that on the range or during a game many golfers will offer you tips. Some are more than happy to give advice when they notice things that you do wrong. I am one of those people who only want tips when I ask for them—not unsolicited. Some people welcome advice anytime. Not me—I would get annoyed when my husband constantly told me what I was doing wrong or how to execute something! I didn't want to hear it. I thought I could figure it out on my own. But in actuality most times I couldn't. It made me more frustrated. I finally realized I needed to listen! I think it's easy to become stubborn because our egos get in the way. Also, people have said it's not so easy learning from your husband/wife or partner. Has this been true for you? Only you know if it is or not! I have learned it's important to get over my stubbornness and *ask* for help when I need it— from someone I trust.

Many people love to give advice, but do you trust them? It's important to find someone you believe in when you want some guidance.

During the grieving process, you need someone just as the golfer does. This doesn't necessarily always mean a coach or a therapist. But I highly recommend it if your loss was tragic or complicated, or any time you feel stuck. It's important to seek help from someone. It could be as simple as allowing a friend to take you to lunch. Perhaps you haven't been out of the house or you haven't been eating! Maybe someone offered to go to the grocery store for you. Many times, people don't want to have others do things for them, but during grief receiving help is important. I have written a three-step guide to help you start your journey of recovery. The first step is to *seek help*, the second is to *receive love* and the third is to *trust yourself.* You can learn more and get this free guide when you sign up for my blog at www.robinchodak.com.

Teachers, coaches, and mentors are crucial to us. They add value to many aspects of our lives, and sometimes they are literally lifesavers. When you begin to play golf, it's important to get one if you are serious about the game. **Why?** Because the teacher has already been there and done what you need to do. They have spent countless hours working on their game. They've had to go through their own emotional setbacks and sometimes, physical ones; but it didn't stop them. They kept going and that is the reason they landed where they are today. They have learned the techniques and compiled what they have learned to help you. It's the same with grief, and that is why I am an advocate of coaches, psychotherapists, or anyone who helps you understand the grief process. A good coach will help you and empower you. An example would be a situation where your grief is triggered because of a song you heard on the radio. It reminded you of your loved one and put you in a very bad headspace. The result—you stayed in your house for days and found yourself depressed. **Has this or something similar ever happened to you?** In this situation, I would help my clients work through it by asking them questions about the experience with the song.

What about it made you happy when your loved one was alive? What about it makes you sad now? I ask them to make lists for both emotions. In every case, the list of happiness has outweighed the sadness. I then ask them to deliberately listen to the song with the 'happiness thoughts' they listed. I ask them to pay attention to how their body feels. Do they feel relaxed? Light? Cheerful? Etc. It's important to make the body/mind connection in grief just as it is in golf. My clients have found this exercise very helpful. They realized that they could embrace the song with a new perspective and hold onto a beautiful memory. I knew it had the potential to work because I used it on myself many times after my husband Steve died in 2005.

By doing your grief work, you will discover that you can sit with the sadness for a period of time. It isn't necessary to push away the emotions, nor should you. Allow them to come. They won't last forever. After they leave, you are able to embrace the good memories. A good coach or mentor will help you do this. It's the reason I started my own coaching business. I believe it's important to help someone guide you on your journey. Just as it is important that you have a teacher teach you the game of golf. After playing or practicing for some time, you feel comfortable. You realize you no longer need your teacher. You can play on your own, taking all that you have learned from them with you. You may play the game of golf for years and feel satisfied with how you're playing. But, there will probably be occasions where you will need *someone* again, so don't be alarmed. It's usually when you feel you are not playing to your standards or you feel a decline in some area. The good news is—you can get another lesson anytime!

It happens on the grief journey as well. You feel you've been moving forward and are in a good place emotionally, and then a grief trigger hits. It's then that you realize you need another session with your coach. I reiterate to my clients that it is not a sign of weakness; instead, it's a sign of strength. It proves your tenacity to improve your life because during grief your emotions can be chaotic, and you don't have the same logical thinking as you normally would. Did you know your brain is actually affected by grief?

Learn about the Neurological aspects of grief at https://www.ncbi.nlm.nih.gov/pubmed/24923337.

If you have lost a loved one tragically, the effects you experience can be more than falling into a state of shock.

Your brain is changed during grief. Is that comforting to know? To a degree "yes" because it confirms that you're probably not crazy. You may feel numb, depressed, foggy, and out of touch with reality. Ironically, this is actually natural and healthy because you are moving through the stages of grief. The emotions allow you to process your grief and once you do that you can move on to the next stage and continue to move forward.

Don't be alarmed if you can't think clearly. It is your brain's reaction to a tragedy. The loss in your life functions as a stressor and triggers the pituitary gland to produce adrenocorticotropic hormone (ACTH), which sends signals to the adrenal gland to release cortisol. Cortisol is a stress hormone. During grief, it's released into the body in excess amounts. Too much cortisol causes the immune system to falter. It's the reason you may become sick. It also may be an explanation as to why an elderly remaining spouse dies shortly after their loved one. Their immune system has been comprised due to excess cortisol.

After your loved one's death, did you ever feel fearful that something bad was going to happen to someone you cared about? Did you feel that your fears seemed to rule you? That definitely was me. I often felt fearful when my mom didn't answer her phone—I imagined something bad had happened to her. I felt the same way with my daughter and at times fell into a state of panic. These feelings do not make you crazy and are the result of your brain function. It is your anterior cingulate cortex that becomes overactive in your brain. During times of grief, the overactive areas of your brain called the *fear centers* are at work—the reason for unwarranted fears.

The higher cortical area of the brain called the anterior cingulated cortex (ACC) helps regulate emotions. During grief it becomes underactive, therefore making it difficult to deal with even minor annoyances. No wonder you feel your emotions are out of control! This short published story depicts my brain after loss.

No Re-write by Robin Chodak

The sun brightly peeks through the edges of the closed window shade in my bedroom. My mind searches for a time reference. It must be late morning. I lie still on the mattress. Getting up requires more strength than I have within me. It's been days, weeks, or perhaps even months. My brain is foggy. With great effort, I pull myself out of bed and grab the crumpled pile of clothes off the dusty hardwood floor and put them on. On autopilot, I head down the stairs while I listen to them noisily creak. I snatch up my keys from the kitchen counter and throw my purse over my shoulder. My body finds its way to the car in the garage. The car seems to have a built-in sensor that gets me to my destination.

I arrive at my stop and once inside, the bright lights make me squint, so I put on my sunglasses. Several people pass by me as I walk. I'm unrecognizable, and that is the way I want it to be. My hat and glasses hide my identity.

As I walk I hope the reason I'm here emerges in my head.

Feeling dizzy, I stop. A grumbling sound roars and a

sudden uncomfortable movement rattles in my stomach. I

grab a bottle of water and sip it. It's hunger once again. I

deny it. No morsel of food has touched my mouth in

days. Only deprivation satiates me now.

I begin to hear voices and suddenly remember the

night my house was crowded with people. Some of them I

knew and others I didn't. Their faces were plastered with

strange looks and their voices sounded hypnotic. It seemed

to be a masquerade party. I closed my eyes and imagined

them away, but when I opened them they were all still there

in my home. Shock vibrated within my bones.

Someone suddenly bumps me, and my water spills.

The memory slowly fades. I continue to walk and finally

remember why I'm here in this place. It's for chalk and an

eraser. I find them and make my way to the isle. I place the

items on the belt. "$11.47 please," says a young woman.

I'm catatonic for several minutes. A man behind me yells, "Lady, I'm in a hurry." I'm unable to focus. Again he yells, "Lady, what's your problem? Cashier, get this crazy lady moving." "Miss, can you please pay?", says the ruffled cashier. "And sir, please calm down." I fumble through my purse to find my credit card and pay.

As I walk to my car I hear a voice, "Take my hand, I can help." "No," I angrily respond. "You can't. No one can. No one understands. Didn't you see how I was treated?"

The voice speaks, "Don't think that you can take an eraser and wipe away your pain and then rewrite what happened. You have suffered great tragedy, but I am here to help. You can take my hand and make me your friend or you can make me your enemy. If I am your enemy, you will live with bitterness and anger and stay stuck in negativity. As your friend, I will help you understand your pain and sorrow. There is no time limit. Everyone processes his or her experience differently. If you trust the process, you will heal. The choice is yours and only yours. You can't deny me. I am, *GRIEF*." My hand extends and I say, "I am ready. I can't face my husband's suicide alone. I need help."

"Yes, you are correct, but you must remember, there are no rewrites, only new beginnings."

The End

That story portrayed my raw emotions after the suicide of my husband Steve. Do not be alarmed if you have had similar feelings; understand it is your brain while processing grief.

Mood swings and sleep disturbances are also common during grief. Do you find that you want to sleep all the time? That certainly was me—tired all the time. I wanted to sleep my life away. Perhaps you can't sleep at all. Or you become overly sad or cry on a dime for no apparent reason. This is your brain reacting to grief. All of these changes disrupt the core functions of your mind and body.

Fortunately, the good news is that acute pain doesn't last forever. It's important to take steps to process your grief, and it's important to take care of yourself and get the help you need.

Dopamine, serotonin, oxytocin, and endorphins are chemicals in the brain responsible for mood, often called the "happy chemicals." Research has discovered ways to boost them.

These practical steps can help boost happy brain chemicals

- Get at least 7 hours of sleep
- Get exercise each day, even if only a 10-minute walk
- Find someone to talk to such as a trusted friend, coach, or support group
- Eat healthily
- Recall fond memories of your loved one
- Eat a piece of dark chocolate daily

- Get and give a hug

I am a firm believer in getting and giving hugs. Virginia Satir, a world-renowned family therapist is famous for saying, "We need 4 hugs a day for survival. We need 8 hugs a day for maintenance. We need 12 hugs a day for growth." That certainly is a lot of hugs. I haven't received that many unless I was at a funeral or a wedding. But, I certainly receive them as often as I can from my friends family. How many hugs are you getting each day?

Why are hugs so good for you? They strengthen your immune system and balance your body. They help increase circulation and help balance your sympathetic (fight/flight/freeze) and parasympathetic (rest and digest) nervous systems. Hugs increase your feelings of safety and emotionally "feed" you. Have you ever noticed how relaxed you feel after a big bear hug? They remind you that you're not alone and you can face any challenge with the person who is hugging you. Hugs increase your feelings of belonging. Believe it or not—hugs boost oxytocin levels, which help heal feelings of loneliness, isolation, and anger. Hugging is a shared experience: you're both giving and receiving affection. Extended hugging (20 seconds or more) boosts your serotonin levels, causing you to feel happy and more positive emotions overall. You remember you're loved when another person looks at you with kindness and affection.

If you live alone like I do and don't have any pets, it's not so easy to get/give all those hugs. I make it a point to hug friends when I see them. Oftentimes, when I have made a connection with someone for the first time, I give a hug at our parting. I may go several days without seeing someone; therefore I've learned to hug myself. **Why not?** It may sound silly but it works; it releases oxytocin and serotonin. This is about your mental and emotional health, so why not do it?

Perhaps you should hug yourself before preparing for a game of golf or a tournament. Give it a try! In addition, it's important to keep your brain healthy too and boost the happy chemicals so you can be at your best!

Many times, the griever doesn't know what to do to take care of themselves and that is the reason I recommend they find someone to help them. We all need someone at different times in our lives to help us grow and evolve.

It's the same for a golfer. They need someone to help them become the best golfer they can be!

Lesson to be learned: Don't let your ego stand in the way. Allow someone to be there for you in your time of need. It will help make you better and stronger on your journey.

Chapter 7: You See Things Differently

You begin to see the game of golf differently than you did when you first began. After playing for some time you actually find you enjoy it. You develop a new way of thinking about it. Actually, you find you like it more than you hate it. **Why?** Because you know you can make some good shots and it feels good. You tend to focus on those more than the bad ones. It's important to think about the game properly. Don't allow chaos to float around in your head while playing, and don't condemn yourself after bad shots. It's important to recognize when you do that. Most of the time, you don't even know that you do it. This is human nature. We tend to criticize ourselves more than we praise ourselves. Our brains are wired that way, and they go on autopilot mode unless they are trained to change.

Don't believe people that say you can't change old habits. Leadership expert John C. Maxwell said, "You will never change your life until you change something you do daily. The secret of your success is found in your daily routine." You certainly can change bad habits into good ones. I offer a course at www.Udemy.com that teaches you how to change your brain and think about grief differently. I help you see it in a new way and, it's called, "Grief a New Way of Thinking." It explains how to make grief your friend. It may sound absurd to you, and that's o.k. Begin to open your mind and think differently about grief.

I had to do it with golf. I would often say, *I hate this 3 wood club or I hate this hole or I never make it over the water*. Making those statements puts out negative energy and my body and mind knew it. Undoubtedly, almost every time I played the hole I said I hated—it ended badly. Every time I used the fairway wood I hated—I flubbed the ball. Every time I was near water—the ball always went in it. **Do**

you see what was happening? I basically created my own errors with my thoughts. Our thoughts create energy that moves us into action. Remember, every good or bad experience you have ever had started with a thought. If you're a golfer—the thought began with the desire to play the game.

The antidote to negative thoughts—say something nice to yourself about your progress. Feel the good feeling in your body. Let the endorphins rise and enjoy it! This applies to golf, grief, or anything in life you experience.

I give my clients three questions for them to think about in each situation they experience during grief. This is Nancy's response.

What am I thinking? (I will never be happy again.)
What is it causing me to do or feel? (Not socialize and I feel sad a lot.)
What am I saying to myself and to others? (Life stinks.)

Below are John's(my client) responses to his golf game.

What am I thinking? (My short game stinks.)

What is it causing me to do or feel? (I tense my body. My wrists feel tight during a chip shot.)

What am I saying to myself and to others? (I don't have any short game in me.)

You can ask and answer those questions in all areas of your life. After you do it for some time, it becomes ingrained, and you become cognizant of your thoughts in relation to your feelings and actions. Give it a try with any situation in your life. Do it with your grief, your golf, or anything else such as diet! It will make a difference.

Write the 3 questions on paper. Writing things down is very important and helps you focus more on what you want to achieve. Keep the paper in a place that you will see every day to keep it in the forefront of your mind. Self-improvement gurus such as Tony Robbins, Zig Ziglar, and

Brian Tracy teach the importance of writing things on paper for goal setting. You can do the same.

An example is a woman named Donna who wants to shed weight. I tell my clients, *never use the word **lose.*** **Why?** Think about it; if you *lose* your keys, you want to find them. You certainly don't want to find the *lost weight*—choose your words wisely. It's a reminder to be impeccable with your word.

Below are Nancy's responses to the questions.

What am I thinking? (I am fat.)

What is it causing me to do or feel? (I overeat and eat unhealthily. I feel bad afterward.)

What is it causing me to say to myself and others? (I can't lose weight. I try but it doesn't work.)

I teach my clients to reframe their thoughts and write their desired answers. These are Donna's desired answers.

What am I thinking? (I want to be a healthy weight.)

What is it causing me to do or feel? (I eat smaller quantite and feel less bloated.)

What is it causing me to say to myself and others? (I want to work out. I want to stick to my healthy plan.)

That is an excellent beginning, but more is needed. I teach my clients to reframe their answers and say things *as if they already exist in their life.* For example, Donna's reframe would be: *I am a healthy weight. I eat only healthy foods. I workout three times per week. C*an you see the difference? You will see and experience things differently when you reframe your answers in the, **I AM!**

The question you may have is: ***how do you make grief your friend?*** I want you to think about your own true friends for a moment. Are they there for you when you need them? Can you call them anytime? Do they want the best for you? Do you know they love you? Do they tell you the truth and don't sugarcoat it? Sometimes it hurts a little but you know they have your best interest at heart. **So**

what do you do? You trust them because they are your friends. I want you to do the same with grief. Trust *grief* because it really is your friend. It wants to walk beside you and love you and be your greatest teacher.

How do you do it? I want you to take it by the hand and make it your friend just as a true friend wants to take your hand and walk beside you until you feel better. Let grief walk with you every day and teach you what you need to learn. It will go into the inner depths of your soul and help you grow. It reveals those hidden things that cause you to feel emotional pain. They may be things from your recent past or your childhood that you have never addressed. Grief gives you the opportunity to discover them and process them. Don't be afraid of it. It wants the best for you. It will tell you things that may be hard for you to hear, but keep in mind it has your best interest at heart. It wants you to learn and grow, just as a true friend does. It has a purpose for you and when you have processed your emotions and learned what is needed then you say to grief,

"Thank you for being my friend. You can leave now since I can walk on my own. You have taught me what I need up to this point. You have helped me to become the best version of myself. You have been my greatest teacher and for that I am grateful. I know you will always be my friend. Good-bye for now."

Does that seem strange to you? Perhaps. But give it a try. It is what I have done and so have many of my clients. We have allowed grief to become our friend and teach us what we needed to learn. Because of it, we have moved forward and live happy lives.

You can do the same, and you deserve it!

This doesn't mean that you will never have situations that arise that cause you to feel grief. When you do, they are called grief triggers. Remember, grief will return as your friend to walk with you and get you through it. Grief continues to teach you if you allow it.

Lesson to be learned: Begin to see things differently by reframing your thoughts in all experiences when you find yourself thinking negatively. Always reframe with **I AM** statements and act **AS IF** things are already the way you want them to be.

Chapter 8: You are Improving

Y ou are feeling much better about your golf game and you're beginning to see some improvement. It's finally apparent by your score that you have improved. When you started you couldn't break 100 in a round. But now after a year or more of playing regularly, it's happened. Most new golfers would be extremely pleased if they could play "bogey golf"—one over par per hole within a year. If a golfer shoots a 90 on a standard par 72 course, that means they were playing "bogey golf" with an average of a bogey per hole. I refer to beginner or average golfers in this book, not professional ones. Although I imagine everything I write holds true for them as well when they first began. But, I believe that professional golfers have an innate ability, or perhaps it is a gift from God, to play above average. It still doesn't come without a price—they must devote much more time to their game than average golfers. I believe those who golf well have high emotional intelligence. What exactly is emotional intelligence?

Emotional intelligence (EI) or **emotional quotient (EQ)** is the capacity of individuals to recognize their own, and other people's emotions. Also, it's the ability to discriminate between different feelings and label them appropriately. They use emotional information to guide thinking and behavior.

The term first appeared in a 1964 paper by Michael Belch. However, it gained popularity in the 1995 book titled "Emotional Intelligence" written by author, psychologist, and science journalist Daniel Goleman. Decades of research have gone into emotional intelligence; showing it is a critical factor that sets star performers beyond the rest.

It takes a certain type of person to be a professional

golfer or a dedicated one, and emotional intelligence is key! Here are some qualities of an emotionally intelligent person. Certainly, everyone has some Emotional Intelligence. Some more than others, and fortunately, it can be learned. You can also increase your current level to achieve better performance. It affects how you manage behavior and navigate social complexities, and it helps you make personal decisions. It is made up of four constructs that fall under two primary competencies (Personal/Social).

Personal competence is your self-awareness and self-management skills. It is your ability to stay aware of your emotions and manage your behavior and tendencies.

Self-Awareness is your ability to read your emotions and recognize their impact while using your intuition or (gut feelings) to guide your decisions.

Self-Management is your ability to control your emotions and impulses as you adapt to changing circumstances.

Social competence is made up of your social awareness and relationship management skills. It is your ability to understand other people's moods, behavior, and motives in order to improve the quality of your relationships.

Social Awareness is your ability to sense, understand and react to others' emotions.

Relationship Management is your ability to use awareness of your emotions and others' emotions to manage interactions successfully.

How much emotional intelligence do you have? If you find you are lacking in some areas—no need to worry, you can always bring up your score. This applies to golf, grief, and all aspects of your life. Apply the following to improve your emotional intelligence.

- **Manage your negative emotions**

- **Be mindful of your vocabulary**
- **Practice empathy**
- **Know your stressors**
- **Bounce back from adversity**

Take the free Emotional Intelligence test at:

https://www.ihhp.com/free-eq-quiz/

Not only do we have some emotional intelligence, but I also believe we are all born with a purpose or calling. And perhaps golfing is the professional golfer's life purpose. The problem is that many people and situations turn us away from ours. You get conditioned to believe you should find a job that pays the most money. It leads you to go to college to become educated for that vocation. But, you may find you're not happy. **Why?** It's because you're not living your life's purpose. Or you're led to believe you don't have a specific talent, so you steer away from something you love, such as painting or guitar playing. It's those beliefs in your head that keep you from your purpose. The question is—**have you found yours**? Your purpose or calling may not be to play golf professionally, but you can certainly enjoy it and improve.

Eventually, you get to the place in your game where you have made progress. Your driver has gained some yards. Your chipping has been closer to the pin. A time or two you actually chipped one in the hole! You are doing more 2 putts than 3 putts. It's all good—your tenacity has paid off, but you still want to improve more. This is good—it shows your strong desire to keep getting better. Without desire, your golf game won't improve nor will anything in your life. Desire must come first. Your improvement has built your confidence, and at this stage in your game, you are ready to invest in new clubs. You want to buy more expensive ones because they have the potential to help your game even more. It's time to take the plunge—you know you are worth it! Doing it is the next step. You must take action.

Grief is the same—you are ready to invest in yourself because you are worth it. You must take action. You realize that you must create a new identity. There are three influential factors to consider as you do; be aware of *whom* you spend your time with, *where* you spend your time and *what* you allow into your mind. Spend time with positive people who support your efforts, not those who love drama or want to drag you down. Put yourself in comfortable surroundings, and make your home as pleasant and peaceful as you can. Keep your mind free of garbage and negative thinking as often as you can! You are no longer the same person that you were before your loss. Your life has changed tremendously and you must begin to do things that will make you happy and ultimately make you a better person. You want to become better. **How do you do it?** You engage in things that interest you. And sometimes it's necessary to put yourself in uncomfortable situations, such as doing something that is outside of your comfort zone. For example, go play a round of golf by yourself, or go to a movie alone. If you are accustomed to being alone, this isn't difficult, so go do the opposite. Put yourself in a group situation where you are forced to interact with other people, such as joining a book club or a dance class. If you have always done things with someone else, then going to a movie alone may be a big deal for you—now is the time to expand your horizons. I know firsthand that it feels uncomfortable, but you will never have a new experience in life if you don't put yourself *out there* to find one. I tell my clients to think of life as a big *playground.* There are various types of rides to take and things to explore. Don't be afraid of it. Find one you like and engage with it. When you do so it opens the doors for new opportunities. It will continue to improve your life and help you move forward. You may find something behind that door that you never thought you would and—voila—it was something good for you.

Discovering or finding your purpose can happen at any

time in life, and it might occur after your loss. It certainly did for me. After my second husband died, I changed professions from a computer systems analyst to a coach and a writer! Don't make an excuse that you are too old or it's too hard.

You can find your purpose and live it as long as you are breathing.

How do you know if you have found your purpose?

- You feel joy doing what you do.

- Your desire to do it continues.

- You are maximizing your potential in what you do.

- You feel confident.

- You are good at what you do.

- You don't need approval from others.

- You're not worried about what others think about your decisions.

- You let your creative juices flow.

- You feel vibrant and alive.

- You are living your authentic life.

- You contribute in some way to the greater good of someone or something.

- You trust the universe will guide you to your next step.

What is necessary is to always be moving to the next step so you can evolve and become better, just like the game of golf. But it takes work. You must put the time into it.

During the grieving process, there comes a time when you feel you have improved, so to speak. It means you've worked through some of the stages of grief. For example, anger is a stage that many feel after a death. They feel angry that their loved one was taken from them—angry that their life changed—angry that they must start a new life— angry about everything in general and angry that they feel the anger! It can destroy you if you don't find ways to release it. Many times people must seek help to manage and process their anger, but once they have—they've improved! This is what must happen with all the stages of grief. You don't want any of them to keep you stuck! Life is about *continuing* to become better and having the desire to make it so. If the desire isn't there, it won't happen. The desire provokes the actions, and then—improvement comes.

Pat yourself on the back that you have seen some improvement. Processing your grief is a step-by-step process. You put one foot in front of the other and move forward. It doesn't happen overnight, it's one day at a time. Doesn't that make you feel good? The fact that you could let go of the anger is an improvement.

Doesn't it feel good to release any negative bondage held over you?

Lesson to be learned: Acknowledge you are improving, but don't become complacent—keep striving to become better. Be the best you can be in all that you do!

Chapter 9: You are Inspired

You are inspired about your golf game. It was either inspiration from the divine, from someone else, or from yourself. Whichever it was doesn't matter. What matters is that you have inspiration. Mentally, you are stimulated to do your best and you *feel* good doing it. This is a mind and body connection, which is important to recognize. You want your mind (thoughts) about your game to be positive. Always pay attention to how your body *feels* as you play. For example, maybe your legs stiffen during a tournament, or perhaps your wrists aren't flexible while you chip when you're 30 feet away from the pin. Or you may feel butterflies in your stomach when you golf with a particular person, *who knows*? Only you. There are a plethora of reasons for your body's reactions. You need to become aware of *where* and *when* you feel the tension in your body so you can work on relaxing those areas. One way to do it is to name the area that is the issue. For example, say, *my arm is tight*, then tighten it for a moment, then allow your breath to go down into the arm, hold it for 3 seconds, then release and relax the arm. Do it 2 to 3 times. This can be done for any area of your body. Give it a try—it may work for you.

An inspired person often feels compelled to be different and do better than their current state of being. Therefore, they keep the momentum going. **How did you become inspired?** Was it from another person or from something you saw or read? We become inspired for various reasons. I became inspired to write books after my losses in life. The reason I write them is that I want to inspire you to become the best version of yourself. Golf teachers do the same with their students. They want to inspire them to become better.

Many people don't become or stay inspired because they are stuck in their old beliefs and habits. We humans are creatures of habit. The Free Dictionary defines habit as: "a recurrent, often unconscious pattern of behavior that is acquired through frequent repetition." You often don't know you do the behavior, and that's when it can get you into trouble. You run on autopilot allowing your habits to control you. It's o.k. for mundane tasks such as brushing your teeth, getting dressed, and driving to work. You don't need to use a lot of conscious energy for those, but if you want to be a success you need good habits imprinted in your conscious mind to be working for you. Therefore, awareness of any habit is the first step. The next step is to create good habits that fit within your lifestyle. For example, if you want to begin playing golf, you wouldn't join a course that's 60 miles from your home. It's too far to drive there several times a week and would set you up for failure. Create habits that are feasible and will propel success.

Aristotle wrote, "We are what we repeatedly do."

Therefore, don't despair; any bad habits can be turned into good ones. Obviously, golf pros and successful people have created them in their lives. Their inspiration was the catalyst to their success.

For the griever, there comes a time after your loss that you feel different. You may not know exactly what the feeling is, but you like it. I will tell you what it is; *it's the feeling of inspiration.* For example, you decided to start the game of golf, or started to paint, dance, or do something that made you feel excited doing it. It brought a whole new perspective to your life. You no longer felt that you would never enjoy anything in life ever again. That's certainly a normal initial thought. But you have worked through your grief, and you have found enjoyable new experiences. Think about what brought you to this place. You created good habits, probably without knowing it unless you were working with me or some other coach! Those habits will keep you inspired and improving. Ask yourself the following questions, and if you haven't already, begin to create good habits around them.

What is your emotional state of being? Be mindful of how you feel. Is it stressed, overwhelm, or exhausted? Create habits to relieve those negative ones such as meditation, yoga, Reiki, spending time in nature, etc.

What is your physical state of being? Are you overweight? Underweight? What does your diet consist of? Create a healthy eating and exercise program.

What is your spiritual state of being? This doesn't necessarily mean religion. Do you feel you have a purpose and inner peace?

What is your social life like? We are creatures that must have interaction with others. Do you have healthy relationships with family and friends? If not, then begin to cultivate them. Meet new people!

What is your intellectual stimulation? We all need various mental challenges to nourish our minds. What are yours? It's important to keep the mind active and working. Learn something new! Find opportunities to broaden your mind.

Small changes have the capacity to turn into large results. Any time you develop a habit, it's important to do it for at least 21 days. Research shows you will have a much better chance of cementing it into your life if you do so. Keep a journal to help monitor your progress. Continue to focus on the things you do right. If you haven't already, begin to keep a gratitude journal. Increasing gratitude in your daily life is a wonderful way to improve mental and physical health, job satisfaction, and overall happiness.

National Gratitude Month occurs in November, and it reminds us that kindness can be one of the most powerful tools for building social bonds and achieving success. There are incredible statistics to back that up.

Why is gratitude so powerful? According to a vast majority of psychologists, researchers, and experts, gratitude is one of the few things that can literally change your life for the better. There is a strong correlation between feelings of happiness, self-worth, and giving or receiving gratitude according to statistics at: https://halo.com/10-amazing-statistics-to-celebrate-national-gratitude-month/

- 70% of employees would feel better about themselves if their bosses were more grateful. 81% would work harder.

- Regular gratitude journaling has shown a 5-15% increase in optimism.

- Regular gratitude journaling increased sleep quality by 25%.

- Gratitude reduces toxins, aggression, frustration, and regret even after negative feedback.

- A five-minute daily gratitude journal can increase long-term well-being by 10%.

- Over 90% of American teens and adults indicated that expressing gratitude made them "extremely happy" or "somewhat happy."

Not only does gratitude help boost general well-being, but also specifically improves self-esteem. A 2014 study published in the *Journal of Applied Sport Psychology* found that athletes who were more grateful had higher self-esteem, which also has been linked to higher performance.

You can learn more about this research at www.tandfonline.com/doi/abs/10.1080/10413200.2014.889255

I understand that if your loss was recent, you don't feel like keeping a gratitude journal. But begin with one thing each night that you can be grateful for, and check below any that apply to you.

My health. My comfortable bed to sleep in. A good cup of coffee in the morning. A hot bath at night. My friends. My garden. The trees in my yard. My home. A good book(this one perhaps).

I am sure you can come up with some of your own. Remember, gratitude is important!

Lesson to be learned: Become aware of any bad habits you have acquired, and begin to change them to good. Continue to do the things that inspire you.

Chapter 10: You Fall Back into Old Beliefs

Y ou hit some bad shots and you fall back into the old thinking that you're not good at the game of golf and won't get any better. If you have injured yourself and can't play for some time, you believe you can't be a good golfer or play at the same capacity you did before the injury. It may be true, but don't presume it is the case. Don't buy into false and negative thinking or the beliefs that will keep you stuck. You must accept where you are with your physical abilities and allow yourself to play at that capacity. Enjoy the game and what you can do with it. You know you've hit some great shots in your game, and you can do it again. Praise yourself for those shots. The reason you play golf is that you know you can hit those good shots. If you didn't believe it, you would be masochistic. You must persevere and have faith in yourself. That's what it takes. You don't want to fall into those old beliefs that have been ingrained in you during your formative years. Many of those beliefs are negative and self-defeating. They don't elevate your consciousness; instead, they drag you down. It's important to recognize when you do that so you can *reframe* as I talked about in chapter 7.

It's easy to fall back into what I call 'stinkin thinkin.' Golf is a game of confidence, and it wreaks havoc with your brain. What is absolutely needed with every single golf shot is complete confidence. Grief is the same; it confuses your brain. The griever must have confidence in himself that he can get through the loss in his or her life. A confidence boost is needed in every single step taken.

Relaxation is also needed when you play the game. If your body is tense, the results you want typically won't happen. As I said in chapter 5, you often feel like a yo-yo. It happened to me recently.

I had the pleasure of hosting a young touring pro-golfer at my house in Florida named Ricky Palonis. He started playing golf at age 12 and is now 27. He realized at a young age that it was something he could be good at—he did what it takes as I've described in this book to get to the professional level. His habits, disciplines, routines, and consistency are the keys to maintaining his success.

On the day Ricky visited, we went to the driving range. He watched my swing and didn't tell me to do anything differently. What he did tell me was key— *I was hitting too many balls*! He said I needed to stop after each shot, get behind the ball and visualize where I wanted to see the ball going. He told me to *think* about that for a minute or two, then walk to the ball and get into my pre-shot routine. Then after that shot is hit—*feel* how it feels in the body—watch the ball till the end. Then realize it's over. It's all about your next shot now. Be in the now with the shot. Wow, that was exactly what I needed at that stage of my game. He also said I needed to set up a pre-shot routine which, like most amateurs, I had not done. Every professional golfer has one!

What is a pre-shot routine? It is a consistent and systematic procedure (a sequence of thoughts, checkpoints, movements, or details) that the golfer executes prior to hitting a golf shot. The pre-shot should start before you get to the ball. It starts when you are walking to the ball before hitting. It's important to create a trigger in which the mind can be conditioned to help you focus. Many golfers use velcroing their glove as their trigger. The act of doing it triggers the mind to put their pre-shot routine in place. You can train your mind to quickly access your shot by asking the following questions:

- How will I play the hole?

- Where is my target?

- What is the distance I want to hit?

- What club should I use?

- What are the hazards?

- What is my intended outcome?

The pre-shot should take between 20 and 30 seconds. Dan Rotella, one of the top sports and golf psychologists said, "Your pre-shot routine is like your wingman on the course."

A fundamental part of the pre-shot routine is to pick a target. First, pick something in the distance, then follow it back to the ball, 6 – 8 inches in front of it—find something there to focus your aim. This will help you line your clubface to the target when you get over the ball. After you established your target, imagine what the shot will look like. If visualization is hard for you, then try to *think* about how a perfect swing feels when you hit your ideal shot. Or listen for the sound that identifies a great shot. Now you can take 1 to 2 smooth swings before the actual execution.

Jack Nicklaus had a habit of doing it in a similar way and was famous for his pre-shot routine. He would start behind the ball and pick one or two intermediate spots

between the ball and the target. Next, he would approach

the ball and line up his clubface to his intermediate target.

Once his clubface was squared up, he would position his

feet and get into his stance. Then he took his shot. Jack and

most good golf players are looking at the golf club, not the

ball. They look at the intermediate target, the primary

target, back to the intermediate target, then to the clubface,

maybe they repeat it, then they hit the ball! Jack never

veered from his pre-shot routine and took meticulous care

in every golf shot!

There is an abundance of things a golfer can do to

prepare for his shot—he must find what works best for him.

After golfing with Ricky, I had increased confidence but

didn't play as well as I had hoped. The next time I went out

to play with people I didn't know, I played the best I've

played in a long time—it felt great! I went out by myself a

few days later; it was cold and uncomfortable—I did

horribly. I wasn't happy. I realized I had lost my confidence. Thankfully, the next time out I remembered what Ricky had taught me and my confidence came back. I played great. It's important to keep the confidence and don't focus on the bad shot you just hit. Put your focus on your next shot. It's all you have at that moment. It's just like processing your grief. If you have fallen or taken a step back, don't focus on it. Instead, focus on your next move and realize all you have is this moment now!

A grieving person may feel like a golfer when they fall into old beliefs about their progress. They feel that their life won't get any better after working so hard on their grief. They may feel that they did all the necessary things but didn't see improvement. Their head tells them, *you aren't strong enough, you don't have the needed desire, there's nothing good for you.* Those are all false beliefs that they must fight off. They need to create a *get-back-in-the-game* routine, just as the golfer needs his pre-shot routine. **How**

do you get back in the game of your life?

Answer the same questions the golfer does in reference to your life.

- **How will I play the hole?**

How are you playing your life? In other words what actions are you taking to create the life you want?

- **Where is my target?**

What actually do you desire in life? What is your target? Is it a job? It is to learn something new? Do you want to make new friends? Do you want to have a loving relationship? You must see your target in front of you. Begin to visualize what you want and see it in action and in color. Begin to feel what it feels like to have what you desire.

- **What is the distance I want to hit?**

Think about how long it may take to get what you desire so you can create a plan of action. How far in the future is it?

- **What club should I use?**

Think about the tools you need to create the ultimate outcome. You may need to enroll in some classes. You may need to read some books—preferably mine! Maybe you need to get some coaching. Identify the tools you need to reach your desired outcome.

- **What are the hazards?**

Think about any potential risks in your path. Are they financial? It is a lack of knowledge? Is it a time or location restraint? Once you identify them—create an action plan to eliminate or work around them so they are no longer obstacles in your path.

- **What is my intended outcome?**

You must know what you desire in your life. No one knows what is best for you but you. Don't let someone dictate your happiness. You have the choice to create your own.

Lesson to be learned: Don't fall back into old beliefs about yourself when things don't go as you thought they would. Focus on what's in front of you and create your unique *get-back-into-the game* routine.

Chapter 11: It's all in your Head

You finally realize that most of the problem has been in your head all along. You know the mechanics of the golf game and you are playing pretty well, but your head is telling you something different.

An example is Karen's experience. She was feeling pretty good about her golf game after playing for 13 years. She played golf with her husband and his guy friends many times and felt comfortable. At least she didn't feel like she was an embarrassment. He had taught her how to keep the game going and pick up the ball when necessary. After her husband Jim died, she didn't play golf for two years. She finally dared to start again and played several times a month with her lady and male friends. She felt pretty good that she wasn't a total disappointment after not playing for so long. But then one day at her country club, she was paired up with a total stranger—Bill. She initially felt nervous but didn't know why because she always felt comfortable playing with her husband's friends.

She pulled up her big girl shorts and chanted, "I will play well." On the first hole she bogeyed it. Her confidence blossomed, and she felt she was off to a good start. On hole 2 her drive was good, but she flubbed the fairway ball. Bill said, *take a mulligan*—she did. That shot went well, but then the next was in the water. She began to feel embarrassed and nervous. She apologized to Bill—to ease her mind he admitted that he wasn't a good golfer himself. She tried to get her confidence back after his little pep talk to her, but she couldn't. She realized it was all in her head, and her body felt it too. Her swing was not her usual one; she was using more arms than hips. Bill then had a few bad shots and confirmed that golf is a mental game. They both laughed!

She tried to focus. She hit some good shots and still some bad ones. She couldn't get her mojo back. She realized she needed to accept where she was and continue to stay calm. She promised Bill that if they ever played again she would be better. She realized that the game was controlling her. Interestingly, after 6 holes they were rained out. It was a good thing because her energy was spent. Basically, the mental energy exhausted her body. In her reflection time at home, she realized she feared the stranger—the unknown. It was more than just the golf game. It was a metaphor for what she feared in life. It was a grief trigger reminding her that she was without a man in her life. She knew she had to work on those negative thoughts because she was ready for a new man to enter her life.

The game with the stranger, Bill, was a new experience for her, and she was glad that she had the chance to encounter it and learn from it. It really was all in her head!

Not only does the game of golf play havoc with your mind, so does your grief, even while you are moving forward. Karen vowed to do some meditation before her next golf game to calm her mind. She also planned to call her grief coach again!

Grief is no different than golf. You will continue to have experiences when your head is controlling you even after you have worked through the stages of grief. It may be because you still have a false belief about it—you think it's your enemy. You think of it that way because of the negative effects you feel from it. But remember that grief is your friend as I spoke about in chapter 7. Grief is a normal experience of life because it enters all facets in various degrees. You grieve because you have loved and lost. The deeper you have loved, the deeper the grieving will be. This is as it should be. As you move forward in life after loss, you will have experiences that are good for you. Then one day you wake up and find that you are happy—wow—it feels great. You float in it for some time and then—wham—you're ready to drown again. Sometimes the drowning is in your head, and you must recognize when that occurs. It's those thoughts that are always swirling in your mind like a hamster on a wheel that you haven't learned how to tame. They are the conditioned beliefs that rule you.

I will give you an example of a client—Rhonda is her fictitious name. Rhonda is a widow. She was married for 12 years to Adam. It was a second marriage for her. Her first marriage to Doug ended in divorce after 9 years. Rhonda and Adam built a great life together, but tragically he died in a car crash. As you can imagine Rhonda suffered from complicated grief. Interestingly, the grief community has identified 17 types of grief spanning from normal to traumatic.

Rhonda came to me to get help processing her grief—which is the first step to start the journey of recovery.

About three years after Adam's death, Rhonda was ready to date again. She knew in her heart that there was still love in the universe for her. She had a big, big heart and wanted to share it with someone. The negative beliefs she once held no longer controlled her. She knew she had a right to happiness again, and she believed she would find it. She took her coach's advice (mine) and approached the dating scene as a big playground. She dated several men. Some were set up for her by friends, others from a dating app, and others she met organically. It felt like a roller-coaster ride for her, and many times she felt she wanted to give up because it was too hard. She wasn't finding that *special* someone. But she remembered the lesson she learned from golf in chapter 3—it's not too hard. And by the way, Rhonda was a golfer, so the golf analogies resonated with her.

Rhonda began to realize that most of the problems she faced were really all in her head. There was one man in particular named Michael that she finally felt different about. In the beginning, it scared her because she hadn't felt that way about anyone since Adam. Michael was different than all the others she had met. There was something about him that intrigued her. He had many qualities she liked. In fact, in one of our coaching sessions, I told her to make a list of 10 things she wanted in a man. She shared it with me and realized that Michael had met 9 out of 10 of them! She also felt very comfortable talking to him about her life with Adam. Everything seemed to be going well for several weeks. But then she began to think she had made a mistake when she talked to Michael about Adam. She felt Michael was no longer as attentive as he had been initially. Her head would spin, and she would replay every conversation she had with him, wishing she said things differently. She often beat herself up, saying *she caused his pull back*. She blamed herself for her behavior. She agonized over it each day because she cared deeply for Michael in the short time she had known him. She was mad at herself for being vulnerable. She started the 'stinkin thinkin' and began to spiral in a head spin.

Fortunately, she had a very close girlfriend who knew her situation. Her friend Gina reminded her that she didn't do anything wrong and that she was being authentic. She said, "If Michael is meant to be in your life, then it will happen. You don't need to worry. Give it time. If it's in the cards for you, then you will get signs. And if not, then so be it. You can't force love." Rhonda knew those things in her head and her heart, but she had lost sight of them. **Has that happened to you?**

Rhonda knew Gina was right, and she remembered those things she had learned during her coaching sessions. She realized how vulnerable she was and that she needed to give herself *grace*. To make Rhonda's long story short— she is with Michael today and has a very fulfilled relationship with him. What she loves the most is that Michael is secure in her love for him. He is not threatened by her past with Adam, and they are both evolving and learning from each other. They plan to spend the rest of their lives together! I love happy endings like that, don't you? Guess what? You can have one too! All you need to do is begin to implement the lessons you've learned in this book.

Perhaps you know too well, as I do, that all endings aren't happy, but I also know that you can create happy endings again with each new experience.

You can also do it with your golf game. You can break 100 or make your next score your best one. That's a happy ending game! You must not let the thoughts in your head keep you from believing it can happen. Remember happiness can be found if you search for it.

Lesson to be learned: Everything starts with your thoughts; therefore it really is "all in your head." Be sure to keep what's in your head positive, keep moving forward, and strive to play your best game in life.

Chapter 12: You are in Control

You are today where your thoughts have brought you. You will be tomorrow where your thoughts take you. James Allen.

Y ou begin to master the head game of golf and now have control over your mind. You know this to be true because you only focus on the current shot—you don't look back at the last one. This has freed you, and your game is so much better—you are extremely happy living in this place.

You have learned that when you rule your thoughts, you rule your world. When you choose your thoughts, you choose your results. The only way to success is to take control of your mind. Allow it to lead you into new places and to see things differently—with new eyes.

If you find that your thoughts begin to control your game or anything in your life negatively, here are some tips to help you regain control.

- Change your attitude about your game/your life

- Change your attitude about a particular person

- Change your attitude about yourself

- Research new interests

- Don't believe it's only done *your way* or *one way*

Do you realize that you change every day of your life? Each thought, experience, choice, and response creates *change* in you. In other words, you will either evolve or devolve in your daily existence. You have the opportunity to change for your good. **How?** By making conscious choices to enhance your body, mind, and soul.

Realize you are always in a state of "becoming what you think." **So what are you thinking?** Even in the midst of difficult times and grief, there is always something beautiful to be found.

Despite what you have learned about how to gain control over your thoughts, you must realize that you are human. You won't always be perfect at it. An example is when you feel nervous golfing with someone for the very first time. **Is that you?** Well, it happened to me recently, and I was upset with myself for it because I thought that I was beyond that thinking! As I said, we are not perfect. Basically, I knew it was *a thing in my head.* I had all these thoughts floating around such as; *am I going to look like a beginner? Am I going to flub some shots? Am I going to look nervous?* A*m I going to feel embarrassed?* Once I realized it was in my head, I flipped my script. I took a deep breath in, held it for four seconds, and let it out for six to calm myself. I then used my mantra—*I am completely confident. I am in complete control of my thoughts.* I recited it silently over and over again until all the nervousness and *stinkin thinkin* left. My body then became relaxed, and I could play the game with ease.

You must realize that the other people in your game are not in control of you! It's the same during your grieving process. You are in control of your thoughts and how you choose to live your life. Widows and widowers need to know this. Oftentimes, they have it in their head that they can never be happy again or find someone that they could love, or someone that could love them. They often feel judged by others. Have you ever heard someone say, *he or she found a mate so soon after his or her loss*. I hear it all the time from clients and they feel judged. It instills in them the belief that they shouldn't find happiness for a long-long time—if ever. This is allowing others to control them and their destiny. **Has this been you?** If so, *what caused you to believe that?* You must remember you can't replace the one you lost, nor should you try. No one can ever measure up to anyone because we are all different. The beauty is that each person you meet on your journey is unique. They have their own special qualities that they bring to this world, and they may be meant to be in your life. Thank

God we are not all alike—how boring would that be?

Don't go into your next relationship with the idea that you're going to find someone like the person you lost. I know this firsthand after losing two husbands. I also have heard Gerry's voice in my head (which I believe is his connection to me in the nonphysical) tell me that I am not to compare him to others. He said, *allow a new special person to come into your life, he will understand you and love you for who you are!* Wow, was I relieved…because someone could certainly feel threatened by trying to measure up to him. Thankfully, I have faith in love and know a special man will arrive in my life just as Gerry arrived after Steve died. I have not given up on love despite all my pain. If you have a story similar to mine—keep the faith.

Golf pros must be in control of their thoughts; otherwise, they wouldn't be a success. Research shows us that successful people have the following qualities.

Passion

It takes a lot of passion to reach one's goals. You must care about what you are doing. Passion can energize you and help push you through difficult moments. Sometimes, people try to fake their passion for various reasons, and when they do, it doesn't get them to their desired destination. A truly passionate person knows that what they are doing is necessary and/or deeply meaningful.

Optimism

Those who start with fantastical goals will often breed the biggest successes. In some cases, those goals have seemed so far-fetched (such as communication throughout the world with zoom). Some would have deemed that impossible. Another example is space travel. But they have become realized, in part, because those innovators held a sense of optimism and a belief in themselves.

Persistence

Being persistent is a necessary quality for successful people. Every successful person has experienced failure—multiple times, and in multiple ways. What separates them from the rest isn't that they fail less; it's that they persist more. When faced with a setback—even a large one—those who succeed don't let it stop them from moving forward.

Creativity

People who can think originally have a greater chance of success. This spans from the arts to the sciences. Every time you are faced with an obstacle, don't go through a logical checklist of ways to solve the problem. Think of any possible solutions to the problem—think outside the box.

Self-Discipline

Many people procrastinate, and everyone has some sort of vice. But successful people never let distractions overtake them. Instead, they have the discipline to keep them focused on whatever they want to achieve, even when they feel the urge to do something less important.

A Desire to Improve

Successful people don't think of themselves as being perfect. They continue to work to improve, even if they have great confidence in their abilities. They identify where they have weaknesses and do what it takes to strengthen them.

A Commitment to Learning

Highly successful people have an amazingly detailed knowledge of their field. And many have an incredible knowledge of other fields as well. Much of their success is the ability to understand the ins and outs of what they've learned and apply it to their vision.

Do you find that you have some of those qualities?
Continue to build upon them to become more successful in
your golf game and your life.

Grievers often feel like the golfer because they
don't know why grief has so much power over them. The
reason is that they have loved. The more you love, the more
you shall grieve. Think about it. If you lose something
that's not important, it doesn't have a big impact on you,
but if it has a sentimental value it certainly will.

Remember, you are in control of your golf game
and your life. Your grief does not need to control you.
Every experience allows you the opportunity to move
forward in life. None of us knows how long we will live in
this physical realm. Therefore, **live, love, and laugh** to the
best of your ability. This is your journey—don't let grief be
your enemy and control you; instead, make it your friend.

I have a personal story to tell about controlling your thoughts. I had a day that some may say—*started out bad.* I had bought tickets to the Honda Classic Golf event to go with a friend in South Florida.

I planned to pick up Kerry at her hotel in Palm Beach. I put the address into my Google maps, yet it took me to the wrong place. I ended up at Australian Avenue and Ocean Blvd. I informed Kerry that I would be late due to the issue. I let Google reroute me. It took me to a bridge that was closed and then rerouted me again. I texted her—*I will be 20 minutes late but at least I get a gorgeous view of the ocean, not a bad price for the delay.* I have the ability to always find a silver lining in seemingly negative experiences. During the amazing ride, my car jolted from a pothole and began to shimmy. I pulled off the road to find my tire completely flat. A park was directly across from me so I pulled in. How fortunate was that? Some call it luck, but not me. I say—*the universe has my back.* I called AAA and they said to put my keys under the mat since I wouldn't be at the car when the tow truck arrived. The call was disconnected before I could finish. I wasn't going to let this keep me from the Golf tournament. I told Kerry I would get an Uber to her hotel. Then the Uber app wouldn't download on my iPhone, and LYFT wouldn't open. I did the normal thing and shut the phone down and turned it back on—still it wouldn't load. I almost gave up the thought of making it to PGA. But then, Kerry said that she would call an Uber for me—that worked! I put my keys under the mat as instructed by AAA and, once in the Uber, called them back. The responder said they couldn't pick up the car without me on site, even though someone had said otherwise. I wasn't going to get upset. I would deal with the car the next morning. After the event, I needed to get an Uber back to my house, and this is the reason I am telling you this story.

I believe the flat tire came to me so I could be in the

presence of the Uber driver. I proceeded to tell him my story and said, *everything that happens to us gives us an opportunity to grow and learn.* Once I said that the floodgates opened. He began to speak like a prophet. He said many philosophical and uplifting words. I was blessed to be in like-minded company. Listening to him gave me hope that people are still spreading positive messages—he certainly was. He was from Jamaica and emoted an amazing quality of positivity and hope. One of the things Donald said that had a great impact on me was, "I never have any bad days—it's just that some days are better than others." Wow, I never heard anyone say that before. It really was a beautiful mindset. He also said, *in life you can either become the victim or the victor from what life hands you*—wow—he was speaking my language, and I felt his strong energetic connection. I told him that I believed I had a flat tire so I could be in his presence to hear those things. I didn't tell him that his story would be in my book, but I believe it needed to be because it is a message for you.

The question is, *can you begin to look at your life as always having good days?* I am not referring to those days after a tragedy or a shock. Those must be processed first. Can you look at your life as being the victor? I certainly strive to do so. This applies to your golf game too. Even if you think that your game wasn't a good one, can you reframe it and say, *all of my games are good, it's just some are better than others.* Wow, that is an amazing thought to strive for, *isn't it?* Can you see yourself as a victor and not a victim? I can. Even though the flat tire was an inconvenience and I had just put 4 new tires on 3 weeks prior, I was proud that I held my equanimity. It's the reason this story is here. I believe the universe gave me the test to ensure I maintain my authenticity. So I say thank you…thank you. It does the same for you. Begin to look for signs in every area of your life and especially after your grief experience. They will come to help you grow and be victorious.

Lesson to be learned: You are the master of your thoughts therefore; you can master grief. Begin to master the Art of Loving Life After Loss.

This book has provided you with ten lessons from golf to help you with your grief. Did you find yourself doing some of the things I have written about? Did you have some of the same thoughts or experiences? Even if you have never played golf can you see that you've been doing the same things that golfers do? I hope that this book has helped you realize that you can learn to love your life after a loss. It's the same with golf. Test the lessons out for yourself. If you have never tried golf and you have the opportunity I highly recommend it. It's a metaphor for how you handle grief and life in general. These lessons can be your greatest teacher. I wish you all the best while playing your game, the game of golf, and the game of life. If you'd like to stay connected go to my website social links at www.robinchodak.com

Love and Light,

Robin Chodak